D0004794

Soothing Your Baby

*Oh, my little baby.
You're so sleepy.*

Try different techniques to comfort your baby, such as holding, stroking, talking, and swaddling.

You learn what works best to soothe her, and she learns to trust that her needs will be met.

THE
CREATIVE CURRICULUM®
LearningGames®

Copyright 2007 Joseph Sparling

Why this is important

A newborn baby's actions are reflexive and her response to her world is very physical. When she feels content, her body is relaxed. When she feels distressed, she expresses it with her voice and through tension in her body. Your baby's trust in you grows each time you respond quickly to her needs. As you determine what calms your baby, you will begin to adjust your response to her needs and reactions. A baby who learns at an early age that her needs will be met cries less as she gets older. Learning to trust you will help her to have trust in herself and others.

What you do

● Pick up your baby and hold her to help her calm down when she shows distress.

● Respond to the tension in her body by swaddling her with a blanket and holding her close so that she can feel your warmth. To swaddle your baby, lay a blanket on a soft, flat surface. Position the blanket so that it looks like a diamond laid out in front of you. Fold down the top corner about six inches. Lay your baby on the blanket with the back of her neck on the top fold. Pull the corner on your right across your baby's shoulder and body, and tuck the edge under her back beneath her arm. Pull the bottom corner up over your baby's exposed shoulder, and tuck it under that shoulder. Bring the loose corner over your baby's exposed arm, across her body, and tuck it under her back. If your baby prefers to have her arms free, you can try swaddling her under her arms.

● Make eye contact, and speak softly to her: *My sweet baby, Mommy's here.* Continue to stroke and cuddle her as she calms down.

● Try making a rhythmic *shhh* sound or turn on a fan or static on the radio to imitate the *shhh* sound. In the first few months, many babies are soothed by a *shhh* sound which is similar to the sound they hear in their mother's womb.

Ready to move on?

As your baby gets older, try comforting her by using a gentle tone of voice and offering soothing touches before picking her up. If she does not calm down, pick her up and comfort her.

Let's read together!

Sleepytime Rhyme
by Remy Charlip

Watching a Toy Go Out of Sight

Jingle, jingle…

Where did it go?

Move a toy out of sight, make a noise with it, and then return it.

Seeing a toy disappear and always immediately return helps your baby begin learning that things are still there when they are out of sight.

THE CREATIVE CURRICULUM® LearningGames®

Why this is important

Babies begin following moving objects with their eyes almost as soon as they are born. They continue to develop this skill as they grow. When you move a toy out of your baby's sight she may lose interest and look away. However, she may continue to look for it if she hears a rattling or jingling sound from the out-of-sight object. She will eventually learn that when people or things go out of sight, they are not necessarily gone forever.

What you do

- Support your baby on your lap so that you can see her eyes. Hold a toy where her eyes are looking.

- Move the toy slowly and notice the way she follows it with her eyes. After a few moments, give her the toy to play with while offering kisses and encouraging words. *You watched Mommy move your keys back and forth and up and down.*

- Keep the game interesting by changing the direction of the moving object and by using different toys.

- Choose a noisy toy and move it out of her sight after she has had success following a toy with her eyes.

- Observe how she reacts when she can no longer see or hear the toy. Make a noise with the hidden toy and then bring it out for her to see and play with.

Ready to move on?

Think of creative ways to make the toy disappear and reappear. The toy can hide under a blanket or shirt, peek behind a curtain, or sit under a hat.

Let's read together!

Playtime Peekaboo
by DK Publishing

Show Feelings

Smile and laugh to show your feelings as you raise your baby and say *up* or lower your baby and say *down*.

Expressing your happiness encourages your baby to join in the expression, too.

Up, up you go!

Down you come!

THE
CREATIVE CURRICULUM®
Learning Games®

Why this is important

When you express your excitement and happiness your baby will be encouraged to join in and show these same feelings. Expressing several basic emotions is not difficult for an infant, but she needs the adults around her to help her learn which emotions are appropriate at different times. When you show a joyful approach to games and learning, your child is likely to be cheerful, too. This activity also encourages her language development.

What you do

- Hold your baby around her chest and under her arms. Smile at her.

- Raise her over your head gently and slowly saying, *Up* or *Up you go*. Lower her saying, *Down* or *Down you come*. Then hug her close to your body.

- Maintain eye contact with your baby as you lift her up and down to help her feel connected to you.

- Smile, laugh, and talk so she can tell by your face and words that you have happy feelings about the game and that her feeling of excitement is appropriate. If this is new to your child, she may look a little worried or gasp when she's lifted high in the air. When she sees you smiling, she will begin to feel good about the movement.

- Go slowly so you don't startle her with movements that are too fast. Give her time to smile and respond to you with cooing or babbling.

Another idea

You can do this activity during routine times of the day such as when you lift her in and out of her crib or onto the changing table, or put her down to play on a blanket.

Let's read together!

Baby Faces
by Margaret Miller

Ride a Horsie

Ride a horsie up and down!

Do a special action on the same one or two words in a rhyme and see if your baby notices.

Your baby will learn to look forward to certain words and their matching actions.

THE
CREATIVE CURRICULUM®
LearningGames®
Copyright 2007 Joseph Sparling

Why this is important

Babies enjoy all kinds of rhythm games. By moving your baby in a special way when you say a certain word in a song, your baby will learn to look forward to the particular word that signals the special event. This helps your baby learn that words can tell her what is happening to her. Hearing a rhyme repeated and moving to it in the same fun way gives her confidence in her ability to predict what will happen next.

What you do

- Hold your baby on your lap as you say the rhyme: *Ride-a-horsie, ride-a-horsie, ride him into town. Ride-a-horsie, ride-a-horsie, up and down.* Gently bounce her to the rhythm of the rhyme.

- Bounce your baby high when you say *up*; when you say *down*, bounce her low.

- Make eye contact with your baby so that she can see your smiling face and you can see what she is feeling during the game.

- Repeat the rhyme and movements several times, then try pausing before saying *up* and *down*. She may show you she knows what will happen next by laughing, kicking her feet, or trying to move her body high and low.

Another idea

Try the game using other songs and rhymes such as "This Is the Way the Farmer Rides," which uses changing rhythms and motions. Choose a special word or words and move your baby in a different way when you sing those words in the song.

Let's read together!

Up!
by Kristine O'Connell George

Reading Pictures and Books

Banana. Yum!

Notice what your baby is looking at in a book and name that picture.

When you name the picture at the moment he is showing interest in it, he will begin to understand more of your words.

THE **CREATIVE CURRICULUM**®
LearningGames®
Copyright 2007 Joseph Sparling

Why this is important

Seeing the pictures and hearing the names of objects on the page help your baby to connect pictures and words. When you place an object next to its picture, you deepen your child's understanding that pictures represent real things. A positive introduction to pictures and books is an important step in your child's literacy development.

What you do

- Collect cards or board books with one simple picture on each page.

- Show a card or picture book to your child and name the object on the page at the moment he looks at it.

- Tell him in simple words about its color, shape, or use: *This is a shoe. A red shoe. You wear it on your foot.*

- Give him the picture to hold and explore, and continue to talk to him about the picture.

Another idea

Pair a picture with an object the baby is familiar with. For example, if you have a picture of a cat, invite him to hold his toy cat as you show him the picture. Talk to him about the object in the picture and the object in your hand: *That's a cat. The cat is furry. You have a toy cat.* Acknowledge his attempts to talk about the picture. *I hear you talking about that cat.*

Let's read together!

Good Morning, Sun
by Lisa Campbell Ernst

Dropping Objects

See the block fall?

Invite your baby to practice dropping things, especially things that make a noise when they land.

Picking up and dropping objects helps your baby gain more control of the muscles in her hands.

THE CREATIVE CURRICULUM®
LearningGames®
Copyright 2007 Joseph Sparling

Why this is important

At this age, your baby can hold things very well but cannot always let them go when she wants. Opening her fingers is a different process from closing them, and learning to control the muscles in her hands will take her a lot of time and practice. Early hand control helps her manipulate objects during play. Later, she will need to control the muscles in her hands when she starts holding crayons and pencils for drawing.

What you do

- Show her a toy in your hand. When she looks at it, open your fingers and let the toy drop.

- Repeat the motion, saying *Drop* as it falls. Keep a short dropping distance so she'll be able to see your hand and the dropped object at the same time.

- Encourage her to try after you have shown her several times.

- Give an enthusiastic response with each attempt she makes. *Wow! You dropped the block by yourself!*

- Play again using a ball that bounces or a bell that makes a noise when it hits the floor. She may show more interest in a toy that produces a sound when dropped.

- Listen for any sounds she makes when she lets go of the ball. This is her attempt to imitate you when you say, *Drop*.

Another idea

Try playing the game during bath time. Dropping objects in the water makes a fun splash that may encourage her to continue practicing her new skill.

Let's read together!

Dear Zoo
by Rod Campbell

Showing What Comes Next

Keys. We're going to get in the car now.

Show your baby a familiar object and tell him what you are going to do with it.

Doing this makes it possible for your baby to think ahead to the next event.

THE **CREATIVE CURRICULUM**® LearningGames®

Why this is important

Your baby will begin to understand what comes next when you first show him a related familiar object. As he associates objects with actions and words, he begins to make sense of his world. The social experience of showing someone something is good preparation for the time later when he will share and take turns with another person.

What you do

● Call to your baby from across the room.

● Show him an object related to what is going to happen next. The object could be a toy, a blanket, a bottle, or a diaper.

● Give him a chance to locate you in the room and turn toward you.

● Hold up the object again, name it, and talk about what is going to happen next. *Here is your bottle. Would you like me to feed you?*

● Try the game when dressing him or bathing him. *I have your lotion. It's time for your night-night massage.* Give him a moment to anticipate the next step before you do it.

Another idea

Expand the game beyond caretaking activities. Show him the vase before you pour water and place flowers into it, or show him a wind-up toy before you wind it up and make it go.

Let's read together!

Ten, Nine, Eight
by Molly Bang

Imitating Actions

You're banging on the pan!

Do some actions that your baby can copy.

This helps him use an important type of learning: imitation.

Bang, bang!

THE
CREATIVE CURRICULUM®
LearningGames®
Copyright 2007 Joseph Sparling

Why this is important

You can take advantage of your baby's natural interest in what you do and encourage him to copy your actions. Providing many opportunities for your child to copy your actions helps him begin to use imitation as a way of learning. Many actions, such as talking, eating with a fork, or driving a car, depend—in some way—on good imitation.

What you do

- Sit down with your child. Hold a spoon and pan, and offer your baby a spoon to hold. Hit the pan with the spoon while saying *Bang, bang, bang!*

- Invite your baby to hit the pan, too. He may bang the pan right away, or he might spend more time watching you before he tries it.

- Offer positive feedback when he tries to bang with the spoon, even if his movements are incomplete. *You did what I did! You're banging with the spoon!*

- Repeat the game with other motions such as tapping the pan with your hands, or using a different object instead of a spoon. Keep the movements simple, and use slow, exaggerated motions that he can follow.

- Try copying your baby when he makes a movement different than yours.

Another idea

Try the game using songs and rhymes with hand motions such as "Pat-a-cake." You can clap your hands once while saying *clap*. You may also try spreading your arms wide and saying *big*. Think of other simple gestures your baby may want to imitate.

Let's read together!

Little Mister
by Randy Duburke

Hi and Bye-Bye

Bye-bye!

Say *Hi* and *Bye-bye* (or *Good-bye*) to your baby, the same way you greet others.

Using standard greetings with your baby helps her learn to wave and say *Hi* and *Bye-bye,* too.

Why this is important

By waving and saying *Hi* and *Bye-bye* to your baby at appropriate times, you provide a model of conversational behavior. By responding joyfully to her attempts to communicate *Hi* and *Bye-bye*, you encourage her to try to repeat those actions. Because the gesture of waving is widely understood, it provides her with an opportunity to communicate with people outside of her immediate family.

What you do

- Smile and say *Hi* when you approach your baby or when she makes an *ah* sound (this may be her attempt at saying *Hi*). Wave to her to get her attention.

- Use greetings during daily routines, such as diaper changing, mealtime, and bath time. For example, when you baby makes the *ah* sound during a diaper change, pause, move closer to her face, smile, and say *Hi* in a gentle voice.

- Observe your baby. She will listen and watch you. She may smile back and then, over time, begin to imitate the sound and motion. Look for signs such as her fingers moving slightly in her lap. She will likely use the hand motion or the sound of *Hi* separately before putting the two together.

- Wave and say *Bye-bye* or *Good-bye* when leaving a room.

- Encourage others to greet her the same way, and help her wave her hand or wiggle her fingers to participate in this early form of conversation.

Another idea

You can help your baby practice greeting others throughout the day. Stand at the door and wave to people walking outside. Greet the cashier at the grocery store or the nurse in the doctor's office and encourage your child to do the same.

Let's read together!

Baby Says Bye-Bye
by Opal Dunn

First Crayons

You made red marks on your paper!

Give your child a crayon and paper and talk about any marks he makes.

Playing with crayons and paper introduces your baby to using tools for drawing and writing. Your words let him know that this activity is important.

Copyright 2007 Joseph Sparling

Why this is important

Crayons provide an easy introduction to writing tools. The simple act of putting a crayon to paper gives your baby a chance to freely explore some of the elements of drawing and writing. He will enjoy moving his arm and hand and seeing the result. Later he will learn to use crayons to express himself creatively.

What you do

- Tape a large piece of paper on the table. Seat your baby at the table and offer him one crayon. He may taste it, feel it, or show it to you. Talk about the crayon. *This is a red crayon. It is smooth and round.*

- Wait for him to make an accidental mark on the paper, or choose another crayon and make a small mark yourself.

- Offer positive encouragement when he makes a mark. *You made red lines with your crayon!* He may make long strokes or just poke at the paper.

- Give him a crayon only when he is seated in front of paper and can freely explore. **Do not leave your child alone with crayons or any other small objects that could be swallowed. Let him explore with crayons only while you are watching to make sure he uses them safely.**

Ready to move on?

When he has practiced with a crayon many times, offer him a choice between two crayons. Eventually, he will be able to choose a crayon from a variety placed before him.

Let's read together!

The Shape of Things
by Julie Lacome

Things to Taste

What's under the lid?

Describe your baby's experiences as she touches and tastes things.

Your baby may connect your words to what her senses are telling her as she explores.

THE CREATIVE CURRICULUM®
LearningGames®

Why this is important

Babies put everything in their mouths because tasting is one of the ways they find out about new objects. After they have tasted and handled something, they decide whether or not they like it. This activity encourages your baby to practice using all of her senses together. Letting her choose from among several tastes establishes positive attitudes toward new eating experiences and helps her learn to make choices.

What you do

- Sit with your baby where she usually eats her meals.

- Encourage her to taste things by putting a few items within easy reach. Try a slice of banana, a spoon, a peeled and very thin apple slice, or a cracker. **Be sure to give only things you are confident your child will not choke on. If you are unsure, save specific foods or this entire activity until your child is older.**

- Let her choose what she wants and let her taste as long as she wants. She may not eat the item, but simply use her mouth to explore. Talk about her choice. *The spoon is smooth and cool. That's a sweet apple!*

- Describe her actions as she makes choices. With each item, she may drop it and try something else immediately or she may show interest in only a single item. *You really like the banana.*

Ready to move on?

When you see that she enjoys looking under objects, try this. Sit at the table with a cupcake pan filled with items of different textures and smells, such as a spoonful of pureed vegetable, a bit of ice pop, or a slice of seedless orange. Lay a lid over each cup. Encourage her to lift the lids and try the contents. Observe and describe her experience with words such as *sweet, cold,* and *wet.*

Let's read together!

My Food Mi Comida
by Rebecca Emberley

Making Useful Choices

Let's go for a walk. Do you want a hat or a towel?

Let your baby choose between two things during an everyday task, one that is useful and one that is not.

Your baby will have a chance to make choices and learn from the results.

It's time to eat. Would you like a spoon or a lid?

Why this is important

Choosing between two objects on the basis of their usefulness is an early step in the process of learning how to evaluate. Adding a few safe choices to his day opens up new possibilities for him to have some control. Making these choices helps him to understand what an object can do and what is needed for a particular task. With practice he can choose the right tool for each job.

What you do

- Give your child two choices of objects to use when he needs to complete a task. For example, if he is ready to drink, let him choose between an empty cup and a full one. When he is ready to eat, offer him the choice of a spoon or a plastic lid. When it is time to wash hands, show him a block and a bar of soap. When it is time to take a walk, offer him a hat or a towel. Let him choose which item he wants.

- Let your child play with the item, even if he chooses the less useful option. Laugh with him as he enjoys the silliness of washing his hands with a block, for example.

- Show him the two choices again and give him a chance to choose more appropriately. *Do you want water? Which cup has the water?* At first, he may choose the less useful object, but with experience he will intentionally choose the more useful one.

Another idea

Add as many choices to his day as you can. Let him feel in control when there is no harm in either option. *Would you like to play with your truck or your fire engine?*

Let's read together!

Wibbly Pig Likes Bananas
by Mick Inkpen

Animal Sounds

The dog says woof, woof!

Make a sound for an animal toy and see if your child can imitate the sound or point to a picture of that animal.

Your child will begin to connect animals with their sounds and their pictures.

Why this is important

Animal names and sounds are useful information in your child's expanding world, and imitating those sounds can be fun. Playing the game with a toy animal and a picture of that same animal helps your child understand that a picture can represent an object. Later, seeing letters next to the animal pictures will help your child to understand that letters stand for sounds.

What you do

- Name one of your child's animal toys and make the sound that animal makes. *This is a dog. The dog says woof!* Repeat the sound and encourage your child to make dog sounds.

- Add a new animal to the game periodically until he knows several animals and their sounds.

- Show him a picture of an animal he knows while also showing him the toy. Remove the toy and point to the picture. Ask him what sound it makes. He may not immediately connect the sound with the picture. *This is the cat. What does a cat say?*

Ready to move on?

Help your child learn the word for the animal as well as the sound the animal makes by repeating the name a couple of times and making the sound. *Dog. Dog. A dog says woof, woof!* Acknowledge any attempts your child makes to say the word. For example, if your child said *Doh, doh,* you might say, *Dog! You are saying dog!*

Let's read together!

Old MacDonald
by Rosemary Wells

Learning to Predict

Where will the ball go?

Toss a ball into a big box or roll it through a tube and then invite your child to look for the ball.

Repeating the game gives your child experience in predicting the outcome of his actions.

THE
CREATIVE CURRICULUM®
LearningGames®
Copyright 2007 Joseph Sparling

Why this is important

When you repeat a simple activity, your child will begin to anticipate what will happen because he has seen it happen before. Repeating the process of throwing a ball into a box helps your child learn to predict where to find an object that has gone from sight. Doing the game again and again helps him learn that he can act in a particular way with an expected result. This builds your child's self-confidence.

What you do

- Find a soft ball and a big box. Stand with your child several feet from the box and throw the ball into it. Ask, *Where did the ball go? Do you see it?*

- Encourage him to look into the box if he does not understand what you are asking.

- Wait for him to notice the ball, and respond with pleasure at his discovery. Repeat this process several times.

- Next, give the child a chance to throw the ball into the box from a few feet away. Respond with enthusiasm each time the ball is found.

Another idea

Try the game using a smaller ball and a tube. Hold the tube higher at one end. Invite your toddler to put the ball in the higher end of the tube. Guide his attention as you play. *There goes the ball! It's coming through the tube.* At first, he may look into the tube to find the ball. After a few times, he will begin to expect the ball to appear at the other end. Hold the tube in different ways to make the ball move fast or slow.

Let's read together!

Peek-a-Who?
by Nina Laden

Make Undressing Easy

You're taking off your shoe by yourself!

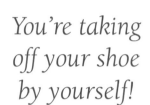

Loosen your child's shoes, unzip his coat, or pull his shirt partly over his head so he can do the last part of the action.

Your child will have the satisfaction of successfully completing the job of removing clothes.

Why this is important

Undressing is a basic part of caring for one's own needs and moving toward independence. Your child may want to undress himself before he has the skills and he may not want you to help him. As he practices this new type of independence, he will be more willing to accept help if he feels he is accomplishing part of it on his own.

- Choose a part of the day when you have plenty of time for your child to practice undressing. It is best if you can make time to practice during a natural undressing transition, such as before a bath or taking off shoes when he comes inside.

- Start with his shoes, because most children are interested first in removing those. Untie the laces and loosen the shoe at his heel so that he only needs to pull it off his toes. Prepare the socks the same way by removing them from most of his foot before he pulls them off.

- Offer positive feedback after each item of clothing is removed. *You took off your shoe! I think you can pull off your sock, too!*

- Undo any buttons or zippers and show him how to pull his arm through the sleeve, when your child is ready to try more difficult pieces of clothing such as a coat or shirt.

- Help with pants by having your child stand and push his pants down to his knees. Then have him sit and invite him to pull them over his feet by himself.

Another idea

Talk about the patterns and colors on his clothes. As he takes off each item, use their names to help teach him the words to describe his clothing. *Red shirt. You are taking off your red shirt.*

Let's read together!

All By Myself
by Mercer Mayer

Water Play

The soap feels slippery, doesn't it?

Without directing him, invite your child to play with water while you say what is happening.

Your child may understand the meaning of most of your words when they describe exactly what he is doing as he does it.

You're good at pouring water.

Why this is important

Young children enjoy water because it moves in unexpected ways. Talking about your child's actions as he plays with water can help him understand the meaning of your words because he can relate them to what he is doing.

What you do

- During bath time, give your child a few toys and talk about everything he sees and touches. *The duck makes a splash when you drop him. The soap is making bubbles on your tummy! See how the warm water goes drip-drip-drip from the faucet?*

- When playing outside, give him a dishpan partly filled with water. Offer him a few toys and plastic cups to play with. Talk about his actions. *You poured water into that cup until it overflowed. You have two hands in the water. You're smiling. I think playing in the water makes you happy.*

Another idea

Find other opportunities for water play. Let him play with water in the sink as you wash dishes, or let him linger for a moment in the soapy water after washing his hands. Talk about what he is doing.

Let's read together!

Splash!
by Sarah Garland

Hide-and-Seek

Oh! You found me!

Move partly out of sight and let your child find you.

Hide-and-seek encourages your child to move around and rely on her own ability to find something that is hidden.

THE
CREATIVE CURRICULUM®
LearningGames®
Copyright 2007 Joseph Sparling

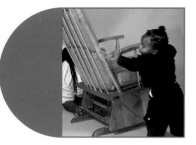

Why this is important

Learning to look for objects she cannot see gives your child a new tool for problem solving. Playing hide-and-seek helps her independently find something out of sight and introduces her to a simple game that she will be able to play later on with other children.

What you do

- Tell your toddler you are going to hide, and then duck down behind a chair or move to another part of the room so that you are almost out of sight. Let her see you go.

- Call, *Can you find me? Where am I?* Offer positive feedback when she finds you and give her a big hug. *You are so smart! You found me!*

- Play together for as long as she is interested. Hide in new places to keep her attention.

- Offer her a chance to hide, and ask loudly, *Where's Carla? Where did she go?* She may hide in the same place you hid. When you find her, act surprised and hug her close.

Ready to move on?

When she is a little older, try playing the game by hiding a stuffed animal in another room. Do not let her see you hide it, but place the toy where she will easily see it. Go back to her and ask, *Where is teddy? Can you help me find him?* Point or give any help your child needs. Show surprise when she finds the toy. *Wow! You found him in the kitchen!*

Let's read together!

Open the Barn Door, Find a Cow
by Christopher Santoro

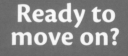

Sing Together

Sing songs with your child, especially ones that she can clap to or that have her name in them.

Singing provides a fun and interesting way to teach your child words and sound patterns.

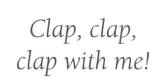

Clap, clap, clap with me!

Why this is important

Your child will become familiar with words, especially rhyming words, through the rhythm and repetition of singing. By hearing the repeated sounds in songs like "Row, Row, Row Your Boat," she will become familiar with the patterns of sounds that occur in language. Singing crosses all language barriers, and when done in a group, singing provides your child with social experiences.

What you do

● Sing with your child when feeding, dressing, walking, or riding. Sometimes use traditional songs and sometimes make up your own. Remember that your child does not care if you sing well. She will enjoy hearing your voice in songs about her and her activities.

● Clap and invite your child to clap with you. Choose a simple, repetitious tune that your child can sing with you and clap to the rhythm. *Row, row, row your boat, gently down the stream. Merrily, merrily, merrily, merrily, life is but a dream.* Your child will first listen, and then begin to imitate the sounds she hears. She may clap and move to the tune before she tries to sing.

● Make up a song with your child's name in it. *Lucy, Lucy, Lucy Ann. I really love you. Lucy, Lucy, Lucy Ann. I really love you* (sung to the tune of "Row, Row, Row Your Boat").

● Try to remember songs your parents sang to you and share them with your child. If your family speaks more than one language, this can be a great way to pass on family traditions.

Another idea

Look for picture books at the library that are based on the words to your child's favorite songs. Sing the song and then read the book together.

Let's read together!

Skip To My Lou
by Nadine Bernard Westcott

Nesting Objects

You're putting the small cup in the big one!

While your child plays with objects that fit together, ask questions and talk about what she is doing.

Your child may begin to recognize differences in size and will become familiar with size words.

Why this is important

By offering her materials of different sizes, you draw her attention to some of the ways objects may fit together. Hearing you describe her actions, she learns words such as big, bigger, small, and smaller. Putting things in order and understanding sizes prepares your child for certain kinds of math learning later in life. As she grows she will use this knowledge to understand ideas such as first, second, and third.

What you do

- Offer your child various household containers in graduated sizes such as juice cans, measuring cups, or plastic storage dishes. Set them in front of her, and then step back and watch her explore them. She may roll, bang, or hide them.

- Give positive feedback when she nests two or more objects. *Look! You put one cup inside the other.*

- Ask her questions about a set of cups by holding the largest one and asking her which one goes in next. Do not correct her if she chooses the wrong cup. Let her experiment with the different sizes.

- Use words to describe the various containers. *That cup is big and this one is small. The small cup is green. The big cup is red.*

- If she appears frustrated, make the game simple by only offering the largest and smallest containers.

Another idea

Look around the house for objects that nest together such as cardboard boxes and plastic bowls. Watch her as she figures out the best way to put items together.

Let's read together!

Blueberry Shoe
by Ann Dixon

Build Together

I made my blocks just like yours.

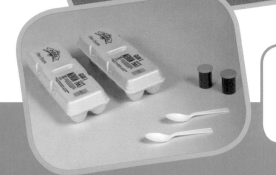

While building with blocks and other materials, copy what your child builds and later invite her to follow your lead.

Your child may become more aware of patterns and learn that patterns can be repeated or varied.

Here are some other things we can build with.

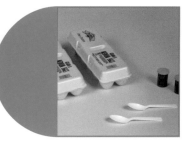

Why this is important

When you copy something your child builds, you help her notice and learn about patterns. Describing what you are doing as you copy her gives her language to describe her actions. If she wants to use the blocks to build what you are building, she will need to listen to words that give directions. Gaining directions from words is an important skill that she will use throughout her life.

What you do

- Sit with your child and invite her to join you in playing with blocks. Arrange the blocks so that you both have a few to play with. Make sure your blocks are similar to hers.

- Encourage your child to begin building with her blocks, and then copy her movements. Talk about what you are doing. *I'm putting my long block on its side, just like you did.*

- Point out similarities between the two finished structures.

- Let your child choose her blocks, and do not insist that she imitate you or build in a particular way. At first, she may not sit still for the game or fully understand what you are asking her to do.

- Invite her to be the leader again, and this time ask for direction as you play. *What block should I use next?*

- Make the game challenging by giving her directions to follow as you build a specific object such as a train. *Let's each make a train.* Build your structure slowly from left to right, and ask her to find each block that you use. *Find your big green block and that will be the engine.*

Another idea

Look for other materials to use for a shared activity. You could string a necklace together or build a fence with sticks. Any matched set of items will work.

Let's read together!

Hands Can
by Cheryl Willis Hudson

Expressing Needs

Talk to your child about what he needs.

Giving him words to express his needs gradually develops his ability to tell you what he needs and wants.

You're hungry. You need your cereal.

THE
CREATIVE CURRICULUM®
LearningGames®
Copyright 2007 Joseph Sparling

Why this is important

By giving your child the words to express his needs, you help him begin to understand that he needs certain things in certain situations. When you ask him about his needs, he has the opportunity to use gestures and simple words to express himself. The more words he can use to clearly express his needs, the more likely his needs will be met.

What you do

- Give your child words to describe his needs. Help your child talk about what he sees and experiences. Here are a few examples:

  You need a spoon for your cereal. I'll get it for you.

  You need a bath before bedtime. Can you find your rubber boat?

  You need a warm coat to go out today. It's cold outside.

- Guess what his needs are by observing his gestures and body language. When he looks or points at an object, try to put his action into words to show him you are trying to understand. *Do you need the doll?* He will appreciate your effort to understand and help him.

- Notice when he begins to use simple words such as *cold* or *hungry* to let you know what he needs. Respond to him quickly to let him know you understand.

Ready to move on?

You can encourage your child to talk about his own needs by asking questions. *Do you have something to put your sand in? How can you reach that high shelf? Would you like me to hold you?*

Let's read together!

Big Dog & Little Dog
by Dav Pilkey

Beginning to Share

This one is yours, and this one is Robbie's.

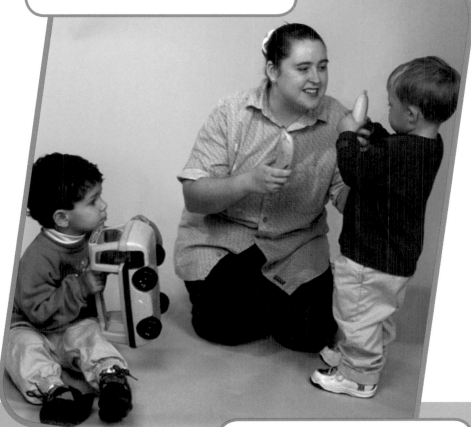

Notice and talk about all the ways your child is beginning to share.

Your talk will give him ideas and words to use later when he begins to form friendships with other children.

Can you give Robbie his banana?

THE
CREATIVE CURRICULUM®
LearningGames®

Why this is important

A toddler does not know how to take turns, divide snacks, or give away toys he wants. He must learn that sharing means giving freely by choice. He may not consistently behave generously for many years, but with practice he will learn early that sharing can be a pleasant experience. Encouraging your child to share feelings and objects with you provides your child with a pattern for later sharing ideas and materials with friends.

What you do

- Model sharing by being physically near when your child plays. Offer to let him park his small car on your knee, or let him hide a block in your pocket.

- Encourage him to share his toys with you by asking questions about them and touching them. If he offers it to you, thank him and hold the toy briefly before returning it to him.

- Help him practice sharing with others by giving him two of something. Tell him one is for him and the other is for a friend or family member. *This graham cracker is yours and this one is for Daddy. Can you give it to him?*

- Make each sharing experience a positive one by focusing on the generosity he shows and describing why it was good to share. *Thank you for sharing the graham crackers with Daddy. He was hungry, too, just like you.*

Another idea

Look for opportunities to share throughout your day together. Your child can pick wildflowers for a neighbor or offer a toy to a pet.

Let's read together!

How Kind!
by Mary Murphy

Exploring Outdoors

> *Do those flowers smell nice?*

Describe the things your child points to or picks up while you play with her outside.

This helps your child to understand the world and learn new words to use as she talks about her experiences.

> *Here's a yellow leaf. Do you want to hold it?*

THE
CREATIVE CURRICULUM®
LearningGames®

Copyright 2007 Joseph Sparling

Why this is important

Playing outdoors gives your child endless ideas for play. Walking and talking with her while outdoors encourages her to explore with confidence. As you describe the things she points to or picks up, you are teaching her words she can use later to talk about her experiences. You are also helping her understand the world around her.

What you do

- Walk outside with your child and encourage her to explore and investigate. Help her feel confident by making sure she is safe while outside.

- Talk about what she sees and touches. *The grass feels cool. That's a prickly bush!*

- Look for any interesting object to share and talk about with your child. *Look at that yellow dandelion.*

- Invite her to safely touch and examine leaves, flowers, sticks, sand, or rocks. She may want you to carry a few items she collects. If she smells a flower, ask her how it smells. When in the sandbox, allow her to play freely as you sit nearby to watch.

- Describe her play using words such as *gritty, sweet, slippery, rough, smooth, scoop, dig, between your fingers,* etc.

Another idea

Add variety to her outdoor play by exploring different places. Simply crossing the street offers new opportunities for your child to explore.

Let's read together!

Pie in the Sky
by Lois Ehlert

Painting With Water

You made a mark with the sponge!

Encourage your child to explore what happens when he rubs a wet sponge on different surfaces.

You will be giving your child a chance to direct his own play and discover that he has the ability to change his environment.

THE
CREATIVE CURRICULUM®
LearningGames®
Copyright 2007 Joseph Sparling

Why this is important

For young children, each new activity provides chances for decision making and creativity. By experimenting with water and sponges, he will begin to notice changes his actions make to the environment. Self-directed play helps your child develop confidence in his ability to make decisions. Holding the sponge and moving his hand and arm in a purposeful way to make marks are good practice for later when he will hold a pencil for writing.

What you do

- Find a place where your child can paint with water and you will not have to worry about the mess. An outside wall or sidewalk work well.

- Fill a bucket, no more than halfway, with water, and find a sponge that your child can easily hold in his hand.

- Show him how to dip the sponge into the water and squeeze before he begins painting.

- Point out the wet surface he creates. *You made a line on the wall!* Allow him to decide what to paint next.

- Notice how your child begins to control his movements in order to direct the sponge in a specific way. He may try different arm movements to create different strokes with the sponge. He might also become more interested in the sponge and practice dipping it in the bucket and squeezing out the excess water. Let him direct the activity.

Another idea

If your child needs a few suggestions of what to paint on, let him try steps, tree trunks, or rocks. In the house, the kitchen floor is a good surface. You can offer him a paintbrush with a bowl of water and let him paint a few toys and plastic dishes.

Let's read together!

Olivia
by Ian Falconer

Trying New Motions

You're taking careful steps.

Show your child how to walk sideways, backward, or across a low bridge.

Your child's skill level and confidence will increase as he learns to control his body while moving in challenging ways.

Why this is important

Your toddler is now able to take on several new physical skills. He will learn that he can move his body in new ways. Learning how to coordinate different motions will help him with activities such as riding a tricycle or swinging.

What you do

- Walk a few steps backward while your toddler watches you. Talk about the movement. *I'm walking backward. Would you like to hold my hand and walk backward, too?*

- Try walking sideways together, or crawling on your hands and knees.

- Make a bridge from a wide board and two bricks. Help him stand on one end, then go to the other end and encourage him to walk to you. Hold his hand if needed, and offer positive feedback when he reaches the other end. *You made it to the other side!*

Another idea

Sing songs to offer another way for your child to try new movements. *If you're happy and you know it turn around.*

Let's read together!

If You're Happy and You Know It, Clap Your Hands!
by David Carter

See, Show, Say

Show me a purple lunchbox.

As you read with your child, invite her to look at, point to, and talk about what she sees on the page.

Reading interactively helps your child stay interested in a book and learn.

THE
CREATIVE CURRICULUM®
LearningGames®
Copyright 2007 Joseph Sparling

Why this is important

Young children who pay close attention to and talk about books are more engaged in learning. Engaging your child in the story helps increase her vocabulary and comprehension, which are important early literacy skills.

What you do

● Sit comfortably with your child to establish a loving reading routine. Pay attention to her eyes as you read a familiar book. If she looks at something on the page when you read about it, pause and describe it. *You see that big, red truck.*

● Continue to read her favorite books to her. As long as she is actively looking and listening she will be learning from the experience.

● Invite her to participate during reading. *There is a bicycle. Can you put your finger on the bicycle?* Or, *Which coat is blue? Can you find the blue coat?* Encourage her to repeat a few words such as *blue* or *coat.*

● Ask questions when she feels comfortable with the book. *What is the little boy holding? Where do you think they are going?* Give your child time to talk about the picture before moving on.

● Think of seeing, showing, and saying as three levels of response to a story, each one more challenging than the last. Start a new book with simply asking your child to notice the pictures. On pages where she cannot name objects, invite her to point. If she can say the names of the objects, ask questions so she will answer with words and not actions.

Another idea

Give your child time to ask questions about the book. Answer her questions in ways that extend her involvement with the book. *The fire truck is going to put out the fire. Let's make the sound of the siren together. Rrrr.*

Let's read together!

Find the Puppy
by Phil Roxbee Cox

Create a Face

And now you're giving her a nose.

Talk about the parts of a face as your child creates one using different shapes.

Your child's self-image will strengthen as she learns how to create a likeness of herself.

THE
CREATIVE CURRICULUM®
LearningGames®

Why this is important

From their earliest days, tiny babies recognize a circle with two eyes and a mouth as a face. Now your child can practice creating her own representation of a face. Using shapes to represent parts of the face helps her learn the correct places for eyes, mouth, and nose. As she gains experience making a representation of a face, she shows that she understands parts of herself and strengthens her self-image.

What you do

- Cut out a large paper circle and a variety of smaller circles or other shapes, and give them to your child.

- Point to the big circle and say: *Let's make a face together. What will it need to see with?* You can suggest some shapes if she needs help.

- Ask what the face needs to eat with. Let her think about what is needed before telling her.

- Offer your child a mirror so she can review the parts of her face. Point out that her eyes are above her mouth and the nose is in the middle.

- Do not change the face your child creates, even if it is incorrect. She will eventually learn where each part belongs.

Another idea

Think of other opportunities to create faces together. You can draw faces with crayons or finger paints. Playing with sand or play dough also offer chances to make simple faces together.

Let's read together!

The Wide-Mouthed Frog
by Keith Faulkner

Dress-Up Play

You chose a hat with flowers.

Talk positively to your child about her choices during dress-up play.

Dress-up play offers your child a chance to choose for herself and develop her imagination.

THE CREATIVE CURRICULUM®
LearningGames®

Why this is important

Most children enjoy trying out various kinds of clothes and seeing themselves in new ways. In this game, your child can decide and choose for herself how to dress up. A child who feels good about herself because her decisions have been accepted will have a more positive attitude in her approach to other people.

What you do

- Give your child a box of simple dress-up clothes and accessories such as hats, gloves, shoes, etc. Make sure your child has a mirror nearby while playing.

- Encourage your child to choose a few items to wear. Talk about the items she chooses. *You are wearing Daddy's red hat! It looks nice with your blue shoes.*

- Keep your comments positive and encouraging as your child decides what to wear on her own.

- Remember that both boys and girls will enjoy this activity. Dress-up play provides your child the chance to experiment freely with various roles without embarrassment.

- Change the items in the box periodically to keep your child's interest, but remember that simple items, such as shoes, scarves, and hats, work well.

Another idea

Expand dress-up time to allow your child to wear her new outfit all day if she wants. Let her know that you value her choices.

Let's read together!

Hats
by Debbie Bailey

Me in a Mirror

Look at you!

Talk to your child about what she sees as she discovers herself in the mirror.

Watching herself in the mirror helps your child connect what she sees with what she feels her body doing.

Why this is important

Your child may enjoy examining herself in front of a mirror. Practicing smiles, making faces, brushing her teeth, or washing her face all help her connect what she sees in the mirror with what she feels her body doing. The more your child learns about herself and what she can do, the more comfortable she will feel in new situations.

What you do

● Give your child a safe, hand-held mirror. **Unless it is a toy made of unbreakable Plexiglas®, you need to stay right next to her to make sure the mirror doesn't break.**

● Encourage her to make faces. *Can you stick out your tongue?*

● Offer her a comb, toothbrush, or washcloth and let her play with them as she watches herself.

● Describe her actions as she sees them in the mirror. *You're washing your nose. The comb is getting caught in your hair!* Make sure you let her direct her own play.

● Use a wall mirror to allow your child to see her whole body. She may pose or dance in front of it. You can join her and talk about her image, but give her time to play on her own.

Another idea

Keep your child's interest in the mirror by offering hats, scarves, or jewelry for her to try on.

Let's read together!

Mirror Mirror What Will I Be?
by Christopher Inns

See It a New Way

Oh, look at this big rock.

Give your child a plastic magnifying glass, show him how to use it, and talk with him about his discoveries.

Using a magnifying glass lets your child see ordinary objects in a new way and increases his curiosity about the world.

THE CREATIVE CURRICULUM®
LearningGames®

Why this is important

Giving your child a magnifying glass helps him discover a new way to look at the world around him. He will discover how the magnifier makes familiar objects look different. With many experiences, he will remember the object as it was and learn how it can look differently.

What you do

- Give your child a plastic magnifying glass and invite him to examine and explore with it.

- Make sure he has a few objects handy to explore. Talk about the differences he notices, using words like *big* and *different*. **Supervise closely when your child handles tiny objects. Watch carefully to make sure your child does not put any small objects in his mouth.**

- Answer his questions and respond with enthusiasm as he shares his discoveries with you. *Wow! There are so many tiny spots on the leaf!*

- Notice how he looks at an object, such as a flower, and then views it with the magnifier. He may take the glass away, look again, and then look one more time through the glass.

Another idea

Let him use the magnifying glass to look at the food on his plate before he eats, or take the magnifying glass with you when you go on a walk together or go to the grocery store. You can offer him another interesting view of the world by using sunglasses or plastic colored lenses.

Let's read together!

Baby Food
by Saxton Freymann

Sharing Nursery Rhymes

Teach your child some of the nursery rhymes you learned when you were young.

Sharing songs from your childhood can help your child learn more about her family's culture.

One shoe off and one shoe on…

THE
CREATIVE CURRICULUM®
LearningGames®

Why this is important

Reciting rhymes with your child provides an excellent opportunity to teach her about the rhythm in language. Using the language and traditional rhymes of your childhood and your family's culture helps your child feel included in a group. Songs and stories are things that many people share in common.

What you do

- Sing your favorite nursery rhymes from your childhood to your child. Make sure to include the favorite nursery rhymes of your family's culture.

- Invite your child to repeat short, simple rhymes. At first she may yell out just a few words that sound alike, but as time goes on she will learn to say more of the words.

- Chant the rhyme to add rhythm. Clap to the beat as you say the words.

Another idea

Invite your child to act out a favorite nursery rhyme. Join in the acting, but let her be the leader.

Let's read together!

Hickory, Dickory, Dock: And Other Favorite Nursery Rhymes
by Sanja Rescek

Color Sorting

You're putting all of the red ones together.

Use two plates and several blocks of two different colors to give your child a chance to sort colors.

Your child will begin to recognize and say color words and sort the blocks by color.

Why this is important

Knowing color names will enable your child to express herself better. As she practices naming and sorting colors, her understanding and vocabulary will improve. Touching the colored block as she names the color will make it easier to remember the name.

What you do

- Gather together a collection of blocks in two colors. Give her a plate for each color and invite her to sort them. *Can you put the red blocks on this plate and the blue blocks on that plate?*

- Talk about her actions. *I see you put a red block over here. Are you going to find another red block to put with it?*

- Offer help if she does not understand the instructions. *This is a red block. Which plate should we put this red block on?* Help her sort a few blocks until she can do it on her own.

- Add another color to the game when she can successfully sort two colors.

Another idea

Look for other items around your house for your child to sort. When cleaning up toys, ask her to find all the green toys first, then the yellow, etc. Or, let her sort cans in the kitchen by matching up the colors. When folding laundry, your child can help by searching for socks with matching colors. Encourage her to name each color she finds.

Let's read together!

Caps for Sale
by Esphyr Slobodkina

Building Blocks

Show interest when your child plays with blocks by talking about his actions.

With blocks, your child can direct his own play and learn about balance by building with various shapes.

You made three things. Can you tell me about them?

THE CREATIVE CURRICULUM®
LearningGames®
Copyright 2007 Joseph Sparling

Why this is important

Your child can make decisions and direct his own actions while playing with blocks, and you can observe how he plays on his own. He may not know where to place the blocks at first to balance them, but he will learn quickly if he is allowed to practice. Your child's self-reliance will increase as he learns that he can accomplish what he tries to do.

What you do

● Give your child a box of blocks of various sizes and shapes. Step back and let him explore and experiment on his own. He may form long, flat lines on the floor before stacking the blocks.

● Limit the number of blocks you give your child at first. Discourage him from using the blocks to throw or hit by showing him how he can use them for building.

● Talk about his creations. *You made something with four blocks. Let's count them, one, two, three, four.*

● Invite him to talk about what he builds if he wants to, but let him play quietly if he chooses.

● Provide comfort and understanding if his work collapses before he finishes. *You are really frustrated that your tower fell down.* Encourage him to try again.

Another idea

Use a collection of cans or small cardboard boxes in addition to building blocks. Your child will have more decisions to make about balance as he builds.

Let's read together!

This Is the House That Jack Built
by Simms Taback

A Fun Path

You're following the path.

Talk about your child's actions as he goes along a path of objects by stepping *over*, crawling *under*, jumping *in*, and climbing *on* them.

Your child's physical skills and awareness of space and positional words will increase.

Why this is important

Following an obstacle course encourages your child's physical development as well as his understanding of the position of his body in space. When you use the words that describe his actions as he plays, it is easier for him to learn new vocabulary.

What you do

● Create a path of various obstacles for your child to move through, such as a cardboard box open at both ends, a small stool to climb on and jump off, or a rumpled towel to step over.

● Use a piece of rope or a garden hose as a guide, if needed.

● Change the path occasionally, using new objects each time. Remember your child's skill level and keep the obstacles manageable.

● Stay close by and use position words to talk about what your child does. *You're going under the bench. You're stepping over the paper.*

● Be flexible, allowing your child to step off the path if he chooses. He may strictly follow the sequence or try different obstacles randomly.

Another idea

Invite your child to play "Follow the Leader." Allow him to lead you along the path as he chooses what to do next. You can be the leader and show him a new way to move around each object.

Let's read together!

Jonathan and His Mommy
by Irene Smalls

Words for Time

Use words about time such as *before*, *after*, or *next* when you talk with your child.

Words describing time help her begin to predict when events will happen.

After your snack, it will be time for a story.

Why this is important

A child this age has no concept of time as it is defined by hours, weeks, and years. She can only relate time to her actions, such as when the blocks are put away, or to a part of her day that is routine, such as lunchtime. Words about time give your child a tool for sequencing events and predicting what will happen next. Understanding time is important for the literacy skill of recognizing the order of events in a story.

What you do

- Use words that talk about time. *We will eat before we read a story together. After our story it will be time for a bath.* Do not expect your child to understand periods of time. She may recognize what is happening now, a little earlier, or a little later.

- Relate familiar events in her life by using specific language such as *the next time we go to the beach,* instead of *next summer.*

- Use time words throughout the day, such as when you go shopping, make dinner, or visit a friend.

Another idea

When reading a book together, talk about the order of events. After reading a story several times, ask a question such as *Which pig's house did the wolf visit first?* or *What happened after it began to snow?* Your child may respond with simple words or by finding a picture in the book that answers the question.

Let's read together!

A Day With Nellie
by Marthe Jocelyn

Cut and Paste

You're making nice snips with your scissors!

Show your child how to make small cuts in a strip of paper or around the edge of a larger sheet.

Cutting with scissors provides a great way to have fun while creatively improving eye-hand coordination.

THE CREATIVE CURRICULUM®
LearningGames®

Why this is important

When a child can use his fingers and wrists well, he can begin to use scissors. Your child will improve his skill in using his fingers and hands through experience with scissors. Children need to know how to use the basic tools of their culture. He will need to know how to use scissors throughout his life, and the fine motor control he develops will be helpful when he begins writing.

What you do

- Offer your child safe, children's scissors, and sit with him as he uses them.

- Let him hold the scissors in a way that is comfortable for him.

- With another pair, show him how the blades open and shut.

- Help him by holding a thin strip of firm paper and letting him snip it. He may cut all the way across the strip and split it into pieces, or he may cut small snips in the edge.

- Offer positive feedback for his efforts. *You cut a lot of snips in the edge of the paper! You're cutting very carefully.*

- Allow him to try to hold the paper as he cuts, but offer more help if needed.

Another idea

Demonstrate how to put paste on the scraps of cut paper and stick them to a larger piece of paper. Let him explore the paste with his fingers.

Let's read together!

Alphabet House
by Nancy Elizabeth Wallace

Help Him Help Himself

You're pouring carefully.

Allow your child to serve himself at meals from bowls or containers that are small or are not full.

Your child will increase his independence as you give him opportunities to do things for himself.

You're putting three carrots on your plate.

THE
CREATIVE CURRICULUM®
LearningGames®

Why this is important

By arranging food and utensils so that he can serve himself, you allow your child to make simple choices about the food he adds to his plate. This also allows him to complete a task independently.

What you do

- Put food on the table in small bowls with large spoons. If you need to use a large bowl, make sure that it is not very full.

- Invite your child to serve his own plate. Show him how to use the serving spoon. Provide a small plastic pitcher and cup so that he can pour his own drink. Be sure to place all items within his reach.

- Guide his choices about which foods to take and how much to add to his plate. Encourage him to eat a smaller amount at first and to take more later if he still wants it. *I see you put three small carrots on your plate. After you eat them, you can have more if you like.*

- Expect a small mess with each attempt. As his skill develops, he will be able to serve his food more neatly.

Another idea

Letting your child serve himself is not appropriate all the time. The needs of the entire family determine which mealtimes will be most convenient for this learning experience. Let your child help plan meals that will work best for practicing his new skills. Talk about healthy food choices as you plan, prepare, and eat each meal together.

Let's read together!

The Carrot Seed
by Ruth Krauss

Run and Walk Together

Let's run!

Talk about what is happening as you and your child run fast, walk slowly, gallop like a horse, or shuffle like an elephant.

Your child will learn words at the same time he learns to coordinate his body and control his actions.

THE CREATIVE CURRICULUM®
LearningGames®
Copyright 2007 Joseph Sparling

Why this is important

Playing outside provides an opportunity for your child to develop his skills in running and moving. When you talk about each motion, you help him learn the words for his actions. Becoming aware of his body movements is an important first step in forming an intentional plan about how to move and when. Moving quickly from running to walking makes him aware of his body and how to direct it.

What you do

- Go outside with your child and show him a few special ways of moving.

- Exaggerate your walking steps and say, *Look at me walking.*

- Start to run as you say, *Now I am running.*

- Take your child's hand and repeat the motions with him.

- Use the words *run* and *walk* as you perform the action so that your child will remember the difference between the words.

- Encourage your child to invent some special ways of moving such as running in a circle, galloping like a horse, running in circles, or walking very slowly.

- Listen for the words *run*, *walk*, *fast*, and *slow* in your child's speech. Offer an encouraging response when he uses them. *You're right, Jeremiah. We walk inside and run outside.*

Another idea

Let your child lead in a game of "Follow the Leader." Encourage him to try new ways of moving such as walking backwards or walking sideways.

Let's read together!

Run, Jump, Whiz, Splash
by Vera Rosenberry

Tell Family Stories

Mama says, "Let's play Hide-and-Seek." Show me what Latisha does.

Let your child move stick puppets to act out a family story that she and you tell together.

Telling stories will help your child understand the relationships among people in families.

We'll pretend these are our family.

THE **CREATIVE CURRICULUM**®
LearningGames®

Why this is important

Handling the puppets helps your child to see her family as a group. Playing with the family puppets may help her to see herself as an important part of a family. She can use her place in the group and her knowledge about her family members to make up stories using familiar information. Having an understanding of how stories are made will later help her better understand the stories she reads.

What you do

- Collect some pictures of family members and friends to cut up.

- Glue the pictures to popsicle sticks to make puppets.

- Make up a story about the family. Encourage your child to move the puppets around to act out the story.

- Include a few real events along with imaginary events in your story.

- Ask your child questions to involve her in making up part of the story. *What do you think she did next? How did it make you feel?*

- Talk about the adults so that your child can be aware of them as people with feelings and needs.

- Encourage her to tell her own story with the puppets.

Another idea

Show your child pictures of herself as a baby and answer her questions about her life then. Talk and ask about people in daily events, such as going to the supermarket. *Who sat in the grocery cart? Which friend did we see there? Who put the groceries in the bag?*

Let's read together!

On the Night You Were Born
by Nancy Tillman

I See Something That Is...

I see something red, and you can read a story from it.

Give two clues, one about color and one about the object's use, to help your child find an object.

Your child will notice more than one thing about a familiar article.

You're looking carefully…

You found it!

Why this is important

Considering two features of an object requires your child to do a two-step evaluation to identify it. He must also listen to your directions in order to determine the important information. Weighing both parts of your description will help him come to a conclusion as he will do with many evaluations throughout his life.

What you do

● Invite your child to play a simple version of *I Spy* with you.

● Give two hints. The first hint should be about the color of the object and the second should be about the object's use. *I spy something blue. You drink from it.*

● Play the game by facing the general direction of the object. Ask your child to touch the object when he sees it.

● Respond positively to his accomplishment. *Yes, that cup is blue. You can drink from it. You listened very carefully!*

● Repeat the clues if your child chooses incorrectly and offer encouragement. *You're right. That is blue. Now can you find something blue that you can drink from?*

● If you need to, make the game easier by placing three items in front of your child and ask for one of the objects using the same two clues.

Another idea

Keep this game in mind when you are waiting in the doctor's office, visiting relatives, or any place your child needs extra attention. Be sure to choose objects your child can point to, touch, or bring to you.

Let's read together!

Hush! A Thai Lullaby
by Mingfo Ho

Soap Curls

The shampoo makes your hair stand up!

When bathing your child, lather his hair thickly with shampoo so that you can shape his hair in several ways.

Your child will be entertained at bath time and will have a chance to see himself in a new way.

Why this is important

Your child can get more out of shampoo than clean hair. He can enjoy seeing his image change in the mirror. This game can help make your child comfortable and familiar with his image even as things change.

What you do

- Use shampoo to create a thick lather in your child's hair.

- Hold a small hand mirror for him to see his new look.

- Shape the lather and let your child see himself in several new hair styles. Pull his hair up into a tall peak or form many small spikes on his head.

- Watch his response, and take your cue from him. If he laughs, say, *What funny, tall hair you have!*

- Add more hair shapes to the game, or try a soap beard and sideburns.

Ready to move on?

Challenge his hand-eye coordination by offering him a second mirror to view the back of his head. Demonstrate how to hold two mirrors in order to view the back. Offer to hold one mirror if he cannot hold both successfully.

Let's read together!

The Hair Book
by Todd Parr

Seeing Feelings

Talk with your child about what people around him are feeling.

Naming the emotions your child sees helps him begin to recognize and understand them.

Do you think Tawanda is feeling a little left out and sad?

THE
CREATIVE CURRICULUM®
LearningGames®
Copyright 2007 Joseph Sparling

Why this is important

Children notice people around them expressing feelings, but they do not have the experience to fully understand what they see. By pointing out and naming emotions when they occur in peers, you help your child recognize what others are feeling. He will have more success interacting with others when he begins to pay attention to the feelings of the people around him. Recognizing another person's emotion is one step in the difficult task of understanding another person's point of view.

What you do

- Point out the feelings of siblings or neighborhood children. Draw your child's attention to another child's strong emotional expression: *I think Matt looks very happy now.*

- Talk more about what has made the other child feel that way. *Holding that balloon really put a smile on Matt's face.*

- Move on to a new topic if your child shows no interest. From time to time, continue to point out feelings and to name them.

- Offer encouragement when your child notices someone's feelings on his own. *You're paying attention to other people's feelings. You noticed Sara was sad.*

- Comment on feelings that may frighten your child: *Chris is so angry right now. I'm glad his Nana is there to help him. I think he will feel better soon.*

- Encourage your child to help a child who feels sad: *Harry looks sad—with tears in his eyes. I wonder if it's because he dropped his cupcake? I think I'll see if he needs some help. Would you like to come with me?*

Another idea

Encourage your child to name the emotions he sees, beginning with happy, angry, and sad. The names of other emotions, such as suspicious, frustrated, and excited, may take longer for your child to recognize and say.

Let's read together!

Today I Feel Silly
by Jamie Lee Curtis

Planting Together

Good, you're getting the dirt right in there.

Create a window garden with your child and talk to him about how you worked together to make the window garden grow.

Your child will gain experience in cooperating and taking responsibility.

Here are the things we need for our garden.

THE
CREATIVE CURRICULUM®
LearningGames®
Copyright 2007 Joseph Sparling

Why this is important

Completing one part of a group task is an early form of cooperation. By participating in a family project, your child will learn to be a partner in getting the job done. Those roles will carry over into school and, later, into his adult life.

What you do

- Choose a sunny windowsill to grow a family garden together. If possible, you may create your garden outside.

- Make a list of needed items with your child and other members of the family, and together collect a few things such as seeds, potting soil, water, paper or plastic cups, etc.

- Begin by putting potting soil in each cup. Give your child as many opportunities to help as possible.

- Ask him to put the seeds in the cups. Choose seeds that sprout and grow quickly, such as green peas or any kind of bean. Demonstrate how to push the seed down into the soil.

- Explain to your child that the plant needs time to grow. Talk about how each plant needs soil, light, and water.

- Place a watering schedule near the window. Each person can take turns watering. Let your child check off his name on the schedule after his turn. *You watered the plants when it was your turn. When we all remember our turns, the plants get what they need to grow.*

- Let your child watch and imitate your care for the plants.

Another idea

Talk about how each plant is growing taller. Encourage your child to draw pictures of the plants to document the growth. Create more jobs involving the plants such as making stick supports for the plants.

Let's read together!

Red Leaf, Yellow Leaf
by Lois Ehlert

Compare Two Amounts

Yes, you showed me the one that has less dough.

Give your child something to play with, such as playdough or water, that can be divided into two parts.

You can help your child notice amounts and talk about them using the words *more* and *less*.

THE CREATIVE CURRICULUM® LearningGames®

Why this is important

Recognizing the difference between two amounts is the basis for many math concepts. Your child will enjoy grouping, dividing, and pouring to create amounts she can label with *more* and *less*. Later, she will use her skills to arrange items in a series.

What you do

- Provide playdough for your child.

- Notice when she divides her playdough: *You made this into two different parts. Look, this ball has more playdough and this ball has less.*

- Move the balls around on the table and say, *Point to the one that has more dough. Point to the one that has less.*

- Continue the game by pressing the dough back together and then making a new ball from part of the dough.

- Show her the ball you made and suggest that she make a smaller ball, one with less dough. Describe the balls using the words *more* and *less*.

- Encourage her to use the words by asking, *How much dough does this one have? How much does the other one have?* Help her with the words as needed.

Another idea

Play the game again using two identical cups with water. Your child will learn a new form of more and less by looking at the level of the water in the cups. Then try other materials and containers, such as sand in buckets, air in balloons, or yogurt in bowls.

Let's read together!

Little Rabbits' First Number Book
by Alan Baker

Stories With Three

Can you count the chairs?

When reading books that illustrate the concept of *three*, stop and let your child count items that come in threes.

Your child will gain a fuller understanding of the number *three* by hearing it in stories and by counting.

One for daddy bear…

THE
CREATIVE CURRICULUM®
LearningGames®

Why this is important

Now that your child is 3 years old, he may show interest in objects that come in threes. You can strengthen his concept of *three* by telling traditional stories that are built around the number three.

What you do

● Bring the number *three* to your child's attention by telling or reading stories with threes such as *Three Perfect Peaches, The Three Bears, The Three Little Pigs,* and *The Three Billy Goats Gruff.*

● Emphasize the number *three* in the title: *Let's read the story* The Three Bears. *Look, here are their pictures: 1, 2, 3. Three bears.*

● Count items in the story that are grouped in threes such as the bowls, chairs, or beds.

● Have your child use objects such as blocks, clothespins, or crackers as counters. Help your child practice handling groups of three: *Count out some crackers to show how many bears there were in the story. Yes! Let's put that group over here. Now can you count out more crackers to show how many bowls there were?*

● Encourage your child to do most of the counting and talking as you move through the story or count objects. Play this game with different books and objects to help your child learn that *three* is a word and a concept used to describe three items.

Another idea

Look for books with three wishes, three tasks, three fairies, etc. You can go to your local library and ask for help in finding stories with a theme of *three*.

Let's read together!

The Three Bears
by Byron Barton

Ride a Trike

Describe your child's experience as she rides a tricycle.

You can provide a safe environment and teach her new words as your child learns this fun motor skill.

Good steering! You're riding right down this path.

Why this is important

Riding a tricycle can provide your child with a new way of getting around. She must learn to move the trike and steer at the same time. She must make decisions about slowing down and stopping while riding something that moves faster than she can walk. Use this opportunity to teach her words that describe space and action. Helping her feel safe on a tricycle builds her confidence as she gains control of the trike.

What you do

- Show your child the tricycle, and then leave it in her play space for her to explore when she feels ready. **Make sure your child always wears a helmet when riding. Even when she practices simply sitting on the bike, she can get used to the feeling of wearing a helmet.**

- Notice how she discovers the ways the trike moves. She may sit on it, turn it upside down and spin the wheels, or turn the handlebars back and forth.

- Use words to help her talk about her actions. For direction, she can learn *turn*, *ahead*, *path*, and *guide*. For movement, teach her *slow*, *fast*, *stop*, and *go*. And for the tricycle she can learn *pedal*, *handlebars*, *wheels*, and *seat*.

- Offer ideas about what she can expect when riding: *When you're ready to make that turn, you will need to slow down. Do you think the path between the posts is wide enough to go through?*

- Give her your full attention and occasional direction as she builds her skills. Although it may seem fun to invite her friends to ride along, it is important for her to ride alone while she learns to control the tricycle.

Another idea

Make a few road signs, such as *stop* and *go*, that will help her learn the rules of riding.

Let's read together!

Do Princesses Scrape Their Knees?
by Carmela LaVigna Coyle

Button and Zip

Lead your child through the steps of buttoning and unbuttoning and zipping and unzipping.

Your child will become more confident with her personal care skills of dressing and undressing.

You're moving that zipper up, up, up.

THE
CREATIVE CURRICULUM®
LearningGames®
Copyright 2007 Joseph Sparling

Why this is important

Guiding your child in learning to button and zip helps her learn the skills needed for independent dressing. Children who are struggling to be independent often are unwilling to accept the help they need. By learning the more difficult steps like buttoning and zipping, she will be able to take care of her own dressing at home or school.

What you do

● Give your child a smock or sweater with large buttons and buttonholes. Explain and demonstrate how to put the button through the buttonhole.

● Show her how to push the button halfway through the hole. Then, hold that part of the button as she pulls the cloth over the other half.

● Keep a few garments handy that have easy-to-fasten buttons. Let her practice during a long car ride or while waiting at the doctor's office. Encourage her to button her own clothes when she is ready.

● Teach her how to zip a zipper by letting her zip up your coat for you. Explain how to hold the bottom of the coat as she pulls up on the zipper.

● Resist the urge to finish the job for her. She needs lots of practice to master this skill!

Another idea

Invite your child to practice buttoning and zipping in front of a mirror. Encourage her to show a friend or relative what she is learning.

Let's read together!

Zippers, Buttons, and Bows
by Moira Butterfield

Two-Step Directions

Take the papers out of the box, and then you can use it as a picnic table.

Offer your child directions that ask for two or more actions.

Two-step directions give your child practice in understanding and completing all the parts of a task.

THE
CREATIVE CURRICULUM®
LearningGames®
Copyright 2007 Joseph Sparling

Why this is important

Your child can learn to follow clear, multi-step directions when you give her opportunities to practice. Following directions is very important in school, and people follow verbal and written directions throughout their lives. Participation in most shared activities involves giving or following directions.

What you do

- Use this game frequently and over a long period of time (a year or more) to give your child an opportunity to practice following directions in many situations.

- Make the game relaxed and use a friendly tone of voice so that your child feels encouraged to listen to you. Begin with directions that ask for two actions: *Please find your boots and put them in the closet.*

- Create directions to lead her to a surprise: *Look in the grocery bag, and then take what you find to the table for our snack.*

- Keep your directions simple with two actions at first. As she confidently completes the tasks, add more directions until there are three or four steps.

- Remember to thank her for finishing the task, if appropriate. *Thanks! You did exactly what I asked.* Offer encouragement for a job well done. *You looked in the bag and put our surprise snack on the table! Now we can eat our yummy graham crackers.*

Another idea

Use school words, such as *crayons, scissors, books, tables,* and *chairs,* to help your child prepare for hearing and following directions in the classroom. A few examples of directions she may hear in school are: *Put some newspaper down before you begin to paint. When you get up, push your chair in, please. Take a book from the shelf and then go and sit where we can read a story.*

Let's read together!

Pete's A Pizza
by William Steig

See and Show

The third thing you do is blow on the paint.

Show your child how to use a straw to make a painting and encourage him to explain the process to someone else.

Great! Would you like to show Melissa how to do this?

This experience allows your child to practice sharing useful information with others.

Why this is important

When you demonstrate a process for your child to share with others, he will need to pay close attention so that he can show it to someone else. When he uses words to explain the steps in a process, he is practicing narration, one of the skills in early literacy.

What you do

- Invite your child to watch you make a straw painting. As you demonstrate, let him know that later he will have the important job of teaching someone.

- Organize your instruction into three main parts so they will be easy to remember.

- Explain that first he must put a piece of painting paper down on a few sheets of newspaper. Second, place a few drops of paint on the paper. The third step is to blow gently through the straw to scatter the paint around. This will make interesting designs on the paper.

- Let him decide which friend or family member he would like to teach. Encourage him to use both words and actions as he teaches.

- Review briefly the steps in the process: *Now, what is the first thing you will show?* Continue to talk through the remaining steps.

- Position yourself near the new teacher and student, but do not intervene unless needed.

- Respond positively to both your child and the one he is teaching. *Michael, you explained the three steps so clearly! Jesse, you blew green and purple paint around your paper!*

Another idea

A few other easy-to-teach projects are making a peanut butter sandwich, planting seeds in a pot, and rolling a ball of dough.

Let's read together!

I'll Teach My Dog a Lot of Words
by Michael Frith

Searching for Sounds

What kind of sound could this make?

Find various objects around the house and describe the sound your child can make with each object.

Your child becomes more familiar with his environment when he has the chance to hear and classify sounds.

Why this is important

A surprising variety of sounds can be made around the house. Exposure to these sounds helps your child recognize, label, and describe them. Knowing and classifying everyday sounds are part of your child's growing awareness of the world. Since sounds occur and then are gone, they demand a different kind of thinking and memory than do objects that will remain in view.

What you do

- Walk around the room with your child, and stop near various objects as you wonder aloud, *What kind of sound could this make?* Encourage your child to experiment with the object to create sound.

- Describe any sound your child makes, such as with a pan and spoon: *Listen to the loud* clang, clang, clang!

- Show him how various objects can make different sounds. For example, drop a small, plastic toy into the sink: *I hear a soft splash.*

- Review the sounds with your child at the end of the game: *Let's think about the sounds that we just made and decide which ones were loud and which ones were soft. First, we heard the sound the pan made. Was it loud or soft?*

Another idea

Search for sounds outdoors, listening for sounds you do not make, such as sounds from crickets, cars, or airplanes.

Let's read together!

The Listening Walk
by Paul Showers

Painting With My Hands

You're making a new color: orange.

Invite your child to explore with finger paints as you describe the process and the marks she makes.

Your child may begin to notice the relationship between her hand movements and the marks made on the page.

THE
CREATIVE CURRICULUM®
Learning Games®
Copyright 2007 Joseph Sparling

Why this is important

Finger painting is a fun, sensory art experience. Through experimenting with finger paints, your child will begin to notice the relationship between her movements and the marks she creates. Allowing your child to freely explore the paints on a large, flat surface gives her the chance to develop her creative expression.

What you do

- Put a smock on your child to protect clothing.

- Use finger paint directly on a table with a wipe-clean surface, or use a cookie sheet or cover your table with a plastic shower curtain to protect your table top. Dampen the surface with a sponge and then put a spoonful of paint in front of your child.

- Stand back and enjoy watching your child freely move the paint around on the table. She may work more easily while standing to allow for larger arm movement.

- Observe and comment on what you see your child making: *You moved your arm in a big circle and now there is a circle in the red paint.*

- Give your child one color at a time as she learns how the paint works on the table.

- Later add another color to the activity. Start with a light color, such as yellow, and add a small amount of red or blue. Your child will enjoy watching the colors change.

Another idea

Save a copy of the finished artwork by pressing a sheet of newsprint on the table and then carefully peeling the paper away. This makes a print of your child's table painting on the paper. Lay it flat until the paint is dry.

Let's read together!

My Hands
by Aliki

Matching Among Similar Pictures

Let your child look for one matching pair among several pictures of the same kind of thing, for example, among several pictures of cars.

Your child will begin to notice which pictures are nearly alike and which are exactly alike.

You found the match! Those other pictures didn't fool you.

THE
CREATIVE CURRICULUM®
LearningGames®
Copyright 2007 Joseph Sparling

Why this is important

Challenging your child to observe and make careful choices from among a group of similar items encourages her to pay attention to details. This skill will help your child as she learns to quickly and accurately see the differences between letters of the alphabet, including letters with similar shapes such as *b* and *d*.

What you do

- Cut out pictures of the same kinds of items in a catalog or magazine.

- Begin the game with four pictures on the table. The pictures should be similar, but with only two that are identical. For example, four pictures of coats, two of which are exactly the same.

- Invite your child to play with you as you ask: *Can you find the two coats that are the same?* When she succeeds, acknowledge her achievement: *You found the two red coats that match!*

- Ask your child to hide her eyes as you switch the positions of the pictures, remove the previously matching pair, and add a new matching pair to the group.

- Play the game with the first set of pictures several times before moving on to a new group of similar pictures.

Ready to move on?

Create a game that uses all the pictures. Spread every picture randomly on the table and invite your child to find each matching set.

Let's read together!

A Hen, A Chick and a String Guitar
by Margaret Read MacDonald

Packing My Own Picnic

You're spreading it well.

Invite your child to pack a special picnic lunch and decide what to include.

Packing a picnic allows your child to act independently and learn from his choices.

THE
CREATIVE CURRICULUM®
LearningGames®
Copyright 2007 Joseph Sparling

Why this is important

Your child probably likes to complete tasks on his own. In this activity he can work independently and his mistakes will have minimal consequences. An important thing for him to learn about independence is that sometimes things do not go as planned. Handling the problems of a poorly packed lunch is a gentle introduction to the risks of problems with later responsibilities, such as getting school supplies together in a backpack.

What you do

- Invite your child to join you on a picnic. Suggest that he first pack a lunch to take with him.

- Go with him to the kitchen and point out available items for packing.

- Talk about where he will be eating, such as in the backyard or at the park, and what foods might be convenient to eat there.

- Lay out the food items as you talk, along with several sandwich bags for him to use. Help him remember where to find his lunchbox or a paper bag.

- Stay in the kitchen while he works, but help only if asked. *I'll be here in the kitchen for a few minutes. Let me know if you need some help.*

- Remember that this is an exercise in independence but you can control his diet by limiting his food choices to healthy items only.

Another idea

When you repeat this game, it might help your child if you remind him of the outcome of the previous picnic: *Last time the pudding leaked out, remember?* He still may make a few poor choices, but you can remind him of what he learned from his prior experiences.

Let's read together!

Hungry Harry
by Joanne Partis

Props for Pretending

I'll cook something good to eat.

Stock a box with supplies that encourage your child to imagine herself in different roles.

Your child's thinking may expand as she dresses up to play various parts.

Chef

Doctor/Nurse

Why this is important

You can encourage your child to use pretending as a way of trying out situations she has not yet experienced. Pretending with props lets her practice future situations and make decisions as well as expand her creativity.

What you do

- Help your child collect and store the props she needs to play different roles. If possible, keep a separate box for each set of props.

- Store the boxes where she can get them out easily on her own.

- Try a few of these examples to get started:

A box with...	To be a...
Dolls, cloths, baby bottle	parent
Aprons, pans, spoons	cook
Book bag, notepad, keys	office worker
Tools, measuring tape, safety goggles	builder
Bandages, blanket, toy thermometer	doctor or nurse

- Limit the contents of each box so that your child is not overwhelmed.

- Add to or change the items in the box as you find more appropriate props.

- Help your child get started by asking: *Can you think of a person who would use these pans and spoons?*

Another idea

At cleanup time, ask your child to help put each item back in the appropriate box. She will need to think about what each object is used for in order to determine where it belongs.

Let's read together!

What Do People Do All Day?
by Richard Scarry

Inspect and Collect

I found a bumpy rock!

Over several weeks, encourage your child to find treasures, display them, and talk about them.

Your child will express his personal choices and begin to maintain an interest in things over a period of time.

THE
CREATIVE CURRICULUM®
LearningGames®
Copyright 2007 Joseph Sparling

Why this is important

You can encourage your child to notice interesting objects in his environment and then help him sustain that interest by keeping the found items available as a collection. He will have the chance to make choices, develop his own personal tastes, and maintain a project for a period of time.

What you do

● Notice when your child picks up and admires small objects he finds. Begin by talking about his new discovery: *I see that rock has gray and white specks in it. It'd be fun to save it. I wonder if there are any other interesting rocks around here.*

● Discuss how the gathered items could be saved as a collection. Your child can create a display of his new treasures.

● Try displaying hard items like rocks and shells in a jar of water to make the colors brighter. Place fragile items in the individual sections of an egg carton. Stick feathers in a small foam block.

● Talk with your child about other ways his collection can be displayed.

● Admire the collection often and wonder aloud about other items that could be added to it.

Another idea

Allow your child to dismantle his collection at any time. He may find interest in a new group of objects.

Let's read together!

Flotsam
by David Wiesner

Fork Foods

Are green beans a fork food?

Ask your child about specific foods at meal times and help her determine whether or not each food is eaten with a fork, a spoon, or fingers.

This experience will encourage her to classify things in a new way: how they are eaten.

THE
CREATIVE CURRICULUM®
LearningGames®
Copyright 2007 Joseph Sparling

Why this is important

By talking about foods and how they are eaten at mealtime, your child will learn the names of foods and begin to classify them. She will begin to think about the different ways a food can be eaten. A strawberry, for example, can be eaten using her fingers or with a fork. Working with food and the appropriate eating utensils is part of handling the ritual of eating in culturally acceptable ways.

What you do

- Invite your child to make three charts with you. The charts should be labeled "Fork Foods," "Spoon Foods," and "Finger Foods." Your child can add to the charts by drawing a fork, spoon, or hand under the related heading.

- Place the charts in a prominent part of the kitchen. Go to the chart before each meal and talk about what food you will serve: *Tonight I cooked fish and rice. We are also having applesauce. What will you use to eat the fish: a fork, a spoon, or your fingers?*

- Offer your child a pencil or crayon to draw a picture of the food on the appropriate chart. If you are eating something that comes in a package such as frozen vegetables or cereal, invite your child to cut out the label and tape it to the correct chart. Repeat the process with each food in the meal.

- Encourage your child to think about which foods might belong on more than one chart, such as the rice.

- Return to the chart regularly with your child as she thinks of more foods to add.

Let's read together!

Eating the Alphabet: Fruits & Vegetables from A to Z
by Lois Ehlert

Another idea

You can play a version of the game when you go to the supermarket. Walk through the produce department and look together for a fork food, a spoon food, and a finger food to take home. Talking about foods in the produce section encourages your child's interest in trying healthy fruits and vegetables.

Syllable Jump

Ma–ri–a.

Maria.

Show your child how to take steps or jump to match the syllables of her own name.

She will increase her awareness of the parts that make up words.

Why this is important

The actions of your child's own body can help her pay attention to the sounds of words and parts of words. When a young child learns something through her body as well as her mind she understands it better. Hearing and responding to the smaller sound units in words (syllables) is part of the foundation for reading and spelling.

What you do

- Write your child's name on a piece of construction paper, allowing plenty of cutting space between each syllable. (If all of your child's names are one syllable, use the name of a favorite person, pet or stuffed animal.)

- Help your child cut the syllables apart. Touch the syllables as you say them. *Kim-ber-ly. Grand-pa.*

- On the floor, ground, or sidewalk, invite your child to help you make a row of connected boxes—like a small hopscotch drawing, going from right to left. The boxes can be made outside with sidewalk chalk or inside with masking tape. There should be one box for each syllable in the child's name.

- Help your child put the cut-apart syllables in the boxes going from left to right.

- Explain that you are going to jump into one box for each syllable of her name. As you slowly repeat her name, hop into a box for each syllable. A bunny hop (jumping with both feet) works well in this game.

- Invite your child to try. Hold her hand for balance if she needs it.

Another idea

If your child is ready and interested, let her jump on the syllables of some other words, such as her last name, the name of her preschool, or her favorite food.

Let's read together!

Chicka Chicka Boom Boom
by Bill Martin Jr and John Archambault

When, How, Why?

Why is it so cold?

In daily events or after reading a book, occasionally ask a question that begins with one of the words *when, how,* or *why*.

These questions will stimulate your child to think more deeply about time, processes, and reasons.

THE
CREATIVE CURRICULUM®
Learning Games®

Why this is important

Asking *when, how,* or *why* questions will deepen the level of your child's thinking. To answer them she will need to talk about time, process, and reasons. This encourages her to give longer answers with several parts. Thinking about *how* and *why* are some of the hardest tasks we do throughout life. This early practice can give your child a pattern of successful thinking to follow and to build on as she grows older. When she answers questions during book reading, she is building her early literacy skills.

What you do

● Ask your child *when, how,* and *why* questions during conversation or reading. *When do we eat breakfast? How did you dig that deep hole? Why did the three bears go for a walk?*

● Give your child plenty of time to think about her answers to these challenging questions. Return to simpler questions if she struggles to answer.

● Pause after reading a page of a book together and ask one of the questions, so she can think about the story.

Another idea

Continue to ask questions that gently test your child's knowledge. Many everyday moments such as riding in the car, taking a bath, or drawing with chalk can offer opportunities for question-and-answer sessions with your child.

Let's read together!

Red Leaf, Yellow Leaf
by Lois Ehlert

Move Up Five

One, two, three, four, five.

Create an easy board game that lets your child move a marker as he counts from one to five.

Your child will remember and understand these basic numbers if he has a lot of enjoyable practice using them.

THE
CREATIVE CURRICULUM®
LearningGames®
Copyright 2007 Joseph Sparling

Why this is important

Your child may already know how to count to five, but he may not understand that each number from one to five stands for a definite quantity. He will practice using the words for numbers up to five as he verbally and physically counts out five spaces on the game board. Numbers are used every day by your child, and he will continue to practice counting skills as he grows older.

What you do

● Make five cards that either have one, two, three, four, or five dots on them. Make the dots large enough for your child to point to and count them.

● Find or make a simple path game board with spaces large enough for a game marker to touch each square as your child advances the piece.

● Invite your child to join you in a counting game. Using your path game board and cards with dots to determine the count, the two of you will take turns moving your markers. Explain the game to him: *We'll take turns choosing a card. The dots on the card will tell us how many spaces to move our marker.*

● Practice choosing a card and counting the dots.

● Encourage your child to move the marker in a hopping motion as you play so that each space can be counted as it is touched.

● Emphasize differences in numbers by saying: *Five! That's a lot.* Or, *Two is a quick hop.*

● Stop the game when your child's interest ends, which may be before the game is over.

Another idea

Throughout your day together, invite your child to count out five objects when he sees them.

Let's read together!

Rooster's Off to See the World
by Eric Carle

Build a Person

You can use this button for a nose.

Ask questions that will encourage your child to create a detailed person from playdough and craft materials.

Your child will practice using his fine motor skills while thinking about the parts of a whole.

THE CREATIVE CURRICULUM®
LearningGames®

Why this is important

Playing with playdough will increase your child's skills in using his fingers. Building a person helps him remember which parts make up a whole. This game supports your child's fine motor development while increasing his awareness of how the body is put together.

What you do

● Invite your child to make a person with playdough by offering a box of supplies such as popsicle sticks, toothpicks, buttons, and a variety of other small items. **Make sure that younger children do not have access to the small parts that could be a choking hazard.**

● Ask your child, *Which of these could you use to make a person?* If needed, prompt him with questions such as, *What could you use for the legs?*

● Notice how he selects items and attaches them in various ways to make a body.

● Make encouraging comments to your child, but do not participate in the game. Let him choose and create his way: *Those buttons make round black eyes. I see you're using popsicle sticks for legs. What a creative way to make a nose!*

Another idea

Your child could use his imagination to create farm animals, birds, or pets. If he seems reluctant to start, invite a few friends to play with him. The children may get ideas from one another.

Let's read together!

Parts
by Tedd Arnold

Add to the Tale

They went back to where the wild things are!

After you read a story to your child ask, *What do you think happened next?*

Your child will practice using her imagination to think logically about the future.

THE
CREATIVE CURRICULUM®
LearningGames®
Copyright 2007 Joseph Sparling

Why this is important

By asking your child to talk about what happens after the end of the story, you are helping her establish a new or future idea based on previous events. Your child will have an opportunity to voice an idea about the next logical step in a story. Throughout life we wonder about the future and try to project our ideas into it. Stories, reading, and writing help us do this.

What you do

- Take a minute to reflect on a familiar story after reading it with your child. After *Jack and the Beanstalk*, for example, talk about the fact that Jack now has the treasures and the giant is dead.

- Ask a question that will help her take the story a logical step forward: *What do you think Jack did the next morning?*

- Give her time to think and respond. If her answer does not contain much information, ask questions that may help her elaborate on her idea. Sometimes repeat her words to her so that she knows you are interested: *So he saw the giant again?* She may add more detail to her answer.

- Ask yes-or-no questions if she has trouble continuing the story: *Did he get up? Did he see something out his window?* She may feel more comfortable after you have discussed several stories.

Another idea

Provide crayons, markers, and paper for your child. Encourage her to illustrate what she thinks happened after the story ended. Record her words on her picture.

Let's read together!

Where The Wild Things Are
by Maurice Sendak

Which Is Best?

That tower keeps falling.

When your child faces a problem, offer two possible solutions and let him choose the best option.

Your child will gain experience in considering alternative paths of action.

Let's talk about some ways you could change it.

Why this is important

Providing your child with two possible solutions to a problem encourages him to think about each one before making a choice. With enough practice, considering alternative actions will eventually become a habit for him. Weighing alternatives is a key step in solving problems. Later your child will be able to link this skill with others to solve problems successfully.

What you do

- Encourage your child to pause when he is dealing with a problem. During the pause, calmly and lovingly explain what is happening. For example, if his tower of blocks keeps falling over, say, *That tower keeps falling. It's made you so unhappy.*

- Talk quietly with your child about problem solving. *There are some things that you could do so that won't happen anymore. Let's talk about a couple of them.*

- Invite your child to consider two options for solving the problem. *You could build the next tower wider and stronger at the bottom, or you could decide to build something else – maybe a long train. Which of these ideas would be best for you?*

- Accept any decision he reaches after thinking about both alternatives. If he suggests a third alternative, congratulate him on his creative thinking.

Another idea

Use this process for helping two children solve a problem. When they argue, calmly sit with them, explain the situation, and suggest two courses of action that they can choose from.

Let's read together!

Talk And Work It Out
by Cheri J. Meiners

Today I Can

You can snip.

…and thread the needle.

Over a period of days, teach your child a skill that involves several steps.

Your child may notice her own progress. She will see that difficult skills are learned over time.

…and stitch.

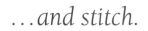

Why this is important

This activity lets your child see that she can now do tasks she could not do before. Learning to see her own progress in a series of steps helps your child set and reach realistic goals.

What you do

● Choose a task that can be broken into short, manageable steps. A few examples are: tying shoes, fastening a seatbelt, setting the table, and simple sewing.

● Gather your supplies. For example, for sewing, you need large cloth squares, thread, yarn, sewing needles with large eyes, and scissors.

● Invite your child to sit with you as you help her with the process and the words.

● Show and say each step: *First, I unwind some thread from the spool and cut it with the scissors. I thread it through the needle and knot the two ends together.* Encourage her to repeat the steps.

● Show the next steps: Sticking the needle in and out of the cloth; using all of the thread; cutting the needle loose.

● Help your child finish. Offer positive remarks for each step she does all on her own.

● Clean up together. Discuss what she did by herself. *Do you remember the steps you did by yourself?*

Another idea

Repeat the task at another time. Review the steps: *Can you remember if you threaded the needle? No? Maybe you can practice that today.* Take pictures of your child working, and make a book with her. She can tell you what she did by herself at each step. You can write her words under the pictures.

Let's read together!

Little Bat
by Tania Cox

Mailing a Letter

Uncle Julian will like getting our letter.

Invite your child to participate in sending a letter to a relative or friend.

Your child will think about people who are far away and have a reason for wanting to learn to read and write.

There goes our letter.

THE
CREATIVE CURRICULUM®
LearningGames®
Copyright 2007 Joseph Sparling

Why this is important

Your child can feel connected to his extended family and friends through letter writing. As he practices reading and writing, he also learns the process of sending and receiving mail. Your child will gain a sense of confidence and connection by understanding that his family is larger than the immediate relatives he sees everyday.

What you do

- Use special family times such as birthdays, national, secular, or religious holidays, or personal achievements to help your child become aware of family members who live in other places.

- Help your child send a letter that could include a picture he draws, a photo, or a card you buy together.

- Show him how to put the card in the envelope, and allow him to attach the stamp.

- Talk about the three items that must go on the envelope before mailing: *This is the address where we want the card to be delivered. That's where Aunt Jane lives. This return address tells that you are the person sending the card. The stamp pays for all of the work that it takes to deliver the letter.*

- Explain the next steps in the process as you go together to mail the card. You might take it to the post office or place it in your own mailbox.

- Talk each day about where card might be on its journey.

- Inform the recipient about the activity and ask her if she would please reply to your child.

Another idea

You can also use e-mail with your child as a way to communicate with family at a distance. Talk about the steps involved in sending and receiving e-mail.

Let's read together!

Dear Mr. Blueberry
by Simon James

Three-Corner Catch

Throw it to me and then I'll throw it to Rohan.

Play an easy game of toss and catch with your child and a playmate.

The children will improve their throwing skills and find that it's fun to take turns and cooperate.

THE CREATIVE CURRICULUM® LearningGames®

Copyright 2007 Joseph Sparling

Why this is important

Tossing and catching is a universal children's game in all cultures. Although your child may miss the ball repeatedly at first, he will learn cooperation and turn taking as he practices tossing and catching the ball.

What you do

● Invite your child to join you in a game of catch.

● Toss a large, lightweight ball back and forth with him a few times.

● Suggest an expanded game. *Brett, let's ask Anita if she wants to toss and catch with us.*

● Introduce the new three-person game. *There are three of us. We can play three-corner catch. Each of us will be a corner.*

● Explain the rules: *Brett will throw to Anita, Anita will throw to me, and I will throw to Brett.* You can walk through the motions to help your child understand and remember the order.

● Encourage success during the game by offering encouragement. *Brett, you threw the ball so carefully to Anita. That helped her catch it.*

● Talk about your own actions as well. *I'll step a little closer to you, Brett. It will be easier for you to catch.*

Another idea

Change the game by adding more players, using a different size ball, or increasing the space between children.

Let's read together!

Night Catch
by Brenda Ehrmantraut

I'd Like Help

Will you please help me open this jar?

Teach your child a phrase to make a clear request, such as *Will you please help me with...?* Encourage her to use the phrase when she wants you to assist her.

This teaches your child an age-appropriate method of enlisting help from others.

Why this is important

Your child has already learned to ask for help in very basic ways. Now she is ready to practice using language that enables her clearly to tell what she needs. Knowing when and how to ask for help becomes even more important as your child's tasks become more complex.

What you do

- Choose a phrase that will be easy for your child to use when she needs help, such as, *I need your help with…* or *Will you please help me…?*

- When you need her help, use the statement or question, yourself.

- Anticipate her need and prompt, *Would you like some help? Tell me what you need help with.*

- Be sure to respond each time she attempts to use her new phrase to make a request. Model language for her if she needs help with telling you what she wants.

Ready to move on?

With your child, role-play times when she might ask for assistance. For example, she can pretend to need help with getting dressed, taking a bath, playing a game, or riding a bike.

Let's read together!

Anansi the Spider
by Gerald McDermott

Let's Imagine

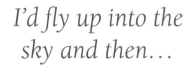

I'd fly up into the sky and then…

Choose quiet times to ask your child questions that encourage her to use her imagination.

This gives your child the opportunity to think creatively by freely choosing and combining ideas in interesting ways.

THE CREATIVE CURRICULUM® LearningGames®

Copyright 2007 Joseph Sparling

Why this is important

Playing this pretend game with your child encourages her to imagine something without any props. Imagining is a way of experiencing something without physical participation. This is a creative way of thinking.

What you do

● Hold your child her on your lap and rock her, or just be close to her as you do during other quiet times.

● Recall a character or situation from a story that you recently read together.

● Ask questions that encourage your child to extend the story, for example, *How did the bear feel when he was on the ice floe? If you had been there, how would you have felt?*

● Offer her an imaginary scenario for her to think about: *If you were going to visit Red Fox, what would you pack in your bag? If you had an invitation to a dinosaur's birthday, what present would you take?*

● Use her experiences to guide your questions. Consider meaningful books, television shows, or recent events that could help her have ideas.

Ready to move on?

Write down her imaginative stories so that you can enjoy them together later.

Let's read together!

Where Do Balloons Go?
by Jamie Lee Curtis

Wondering What Caused It

Look at the new color!

Ask your child questions about the world around him that will lead him to think about why things happen.

As your child begins to link cause and effect, he will think about explanations for changes that he sees.

Why this is important

Your questions can guide your child to think about cause and effect. Asking questions can encourage him to look at ordinary events more closely. The problems we attempt to solve get harder as we grow, but the method of thinking back to what happened before continues to be an effective way to try to understand and solve them.

What you do

- Observe your child's curiosity about events in his day. Almost any daily occurrence can be used for this game. A few examples are water freezing, a broken toy, and leaves falling from the trees.

- Guide him in wondering about cause and effect. Start by saying: *We're going to do some detective work to find out what caused that!*

- Ask questions that help him recount what just happened. *Now let's see. You were painting with two jars of color. What were the colors? Yes, that's right. Red and yellow. Now you have orange paint in the middle. Where do you think it came from?*

- Offer a different idea if his explanation is inaccurate. Do not correct his theory, but simply offer another view.

- Encourage any effort to figure out the cause of the mystery. Your child should feel comfortable exploring all possibilities that he thinks of.

Another idea

Encourage your child to be a detective in discovering what caused something to happen. Give him a notebook, a pencil, and a magnifying glass to use in his investigation.

Let's read together!

White Rabbit's Color Book
by Alan Baker